THE PLEDGE
OF ALLEGIANCE

SCHOLASTIC INC. Cartwheel BOOKS®

New York   Toronto   London   Auckland   Sydney
Mexico City   New Delhi   Hong Kong   Buenos Aires

Photography credits for *The Pledge of Allegiance*:
Cover: John Fleck/Stone; Back cover: Art Montes De Oca/FPG; page 3: Chip Henderson/Stone; page 4: SuperStock; page 5, top left: Chromosohn/Photo Researchers; page 5, right: Philip Spears/FPG; page 5, bottom left: Steve Skjold/PhotoEdit; page 6, top left: Toyohiro Yamada/FPG; page 6, top right: Dennis Flaherty/Photo Researchers; page 6, bottom right: FPG; page 6, bottom left: SuperStock; page 7: Harvey Lloyd/FPG; page 8: Paul Sakuma/AP Wide World Photo; page 9: Owen Franken/Corbis; page 10: NASA/AP Wide World Photo; page 11, top left: Jerry Alexander/Stone; page 11, right: Peter Gridley/FPG; page 11, bottom left: SuperStock; page 12: PhotoDisc; page 13: Robert W. Ginn/PhotoEdit; page 14-15: Art Montes De Oca/FPG; page 16, left: SuperStock; page 16-17: Arthur Tilley/FPG; page 18, background: David Young Wolff/PhotoEdit; page 18, top left: Myrleen Ferguson Cate/PhotoEdit; page 18, right: Philip Spears/FPG; page 18, bottom left: Michelle & Tom Grimm/Stone; page 19: Art Montes De Oca/FPG; page 20, left: Reza Estakhrian/Stone; page 20-21: SuperStock; page 22: FPG; page 23: Michael Newman/PhotoEdit; page 24: FPG; page 26: top row: Chip Henderson/Stone; second row from top left: Toyohiro Yamada/FPG; middle: SuperStock; right: Dennis Flaherty/Photo Researchers; far right: Harvey Lloyd/FPG; third row from top: Paul Sakuma/AP Wide World Photo; bottom row: Owen Franken/Corbis; page 27: top row: NASA/AP Wide World Photo; second row from top left: Jerry Alexander/Stone; middle: SuperStock; right: Peter Gridley/FPG; third row from top: Reza Estakhrian/Stone; bottom row: SuperStock; page 28: FPG; page 31: Owen Franken/Corbis; page 32: SuperStock.

The editors would like to thank Kama Einhorn for her contributions to the endnotes.

ISBN 0-439-39962-9
Copyright © 2000 by Scholastic Inc. All rights reserved. Published by Scholastic Inc.
SCHOLASTIC, CARTWHEEL BOOKS and associated logos are trademarks and/or registered trademarks of Scholastic Inc.
12 11 10 9 8 7 6 5 4 3 2 1   1 2 3 4 5 6 /0
Printed in the U.S.A.   08

First Scholastic printing, September 2000

I pledge allegiance

to the flag

of the United States of America

and to the Republic

for which it stands,

one Nation

under God,

indivisible,

with liberty

EQUAL JUSTICE UNDER LAW

and justice

for all.

Turn the page for facts about the Pledge of Allegiance and the American Flag!

About These Photos:

When Americans recite the Pledge of Allegiance, we place our hands on our hearts to show we mean what we say.

These pictures show some of the landscapes in the United States.

Monument Valley is in Utah.

This lighthouse is in Portland, Maine.

This barn is in the state of Washington.

These mountains are in Lake Powell, Arizona.

This is the world's largest American flag. It is 255 feet wide by 505 feet long. It was unfurled for display on Flag Day, June 14, 1998, at Moffett Field Air Station in California.

The first American flag was made in 1776. The 13 stars in a circle stand for the 13 original colonies: Massachusetts, Connecticut, Rhode Island, New Hampshire, New York, New Jersey, Pennsylvania, Delaware, Virginia, Maryland, North Carolina, South Carolina, and Georgia.

 In 1969, American astronaut Neil Armstrong left an American flag on the moon.

These landmarks are all located in Washington, D.C., the capital of the United States.

The Washington Monument was built to honor George Washington, the first president of the United States.

The Lincoln Memorial was built to honor Abraham Lincoln, the 16th president of the United States.

The dome of the U. S. Capitol Building. Members of Congress meet in this building to make the laws of our nation.

 This is the statue of Justice. In her left hand, the statue holds scales, which represent the decision between right and wrong. In her right hand, she holds a sword, which represents punishment for a crime. The statue is wearing a blindfold to show that justice does not favor one person over another.

 This flag is flying only halfway up the flagpole. When important Americans die, we fly the flag at half-mast as a sign of mourning.

The Pledge of Allegiance was written in 1892 for a children's magazine called *The Youth's Companion* by Francis Bellamy who hoped that his words would give children a sense of pride and love for their country.

What Does the Pledge of Allegiance Mean?

I pledge allegiance to the flag of the United States of America…

When we "pledge allegiance," we promise to be loyal to our country.

and to the Republic for which it stands…

Our government is called a Republic. In a Republic, people vote in elections in which leaders are chosen to run the government and make laws that affect every citizen.

one Nation under God, indivisible…

The United States cannot be divided.

with liberty and justice for all.

All Americans should have the same freedoms and should be treated fairly.

Days to Display the Flag:

The flag should be displayed from sunrise to sunset, weather permitting, on the following special days:

- ✪ New Year's Day, January 1
- ✪ Inauguration Day, January 20
- ✪ Martin Luther King, Jr. Day, third Monday in January
- ✪ Lincoln's Birthday, February 12
- ✪ Washington's Birthday/President's Day, third Monday in February
- ✪ Patriots' Day, April 19
- ✪ Mother's Day, second Sunday in May
- ✪ Armed Forces Day, third Saturday in May
- ✪ Memorial Day, fourth Monday in May (half-mast until noon)
- ✪ Flag Day, June 14
- ✪ Independence Day, July 4
- ✪ Labor Day, first Monday in September
- ✪ Constitution Day, September 17
- ✪ National POW/MIA Recognition Day, September 19
- ✪ Columbus Day, second Monday in October
- ✪ Navy Day, October 27
- ✪ Veterans Day, November 11
- ✪ Thanksgiving Day, fourth Thursday in November

Did You Know…

- ★ Betsy Ross sat near George Washington in church.
- ★ When a flag gets too old to display, it is burned in a special ceremony.
- ★ No one knows what happened to the first flag.
- ★ The flag has a nickname — "Old Glory."
- ★ A flag should never touch the ground.
- ★ When the President is not in Washington, D.C., the flag outside the White House doesn't fly!
- ★ There is always a flag hanging where people vote.

The First United States Flag

The first flag is believed to have been designed by Francis Hopkinson and sewn by Betsy Ross, a seamstress from Philadelphia.

The stars and stripes on the first flag stood for the first 13 colonies. These colonies later became states.

The stars were arranged in a circle to show that every colony was equal.

Our Flag Today

Our flag looks different from the one that was first made in 1776.

Now there are 50 stars, one for each of the 50 states.
The 13 stripes help us remember the first 13 colonies.
Red stands for bravery; White stands for liberty;
Blue stands for justice.